IF I WERE TO DO IT AGAIN

Forty two years in the gospel ministry

JOSEPH K. DUBE

ISBN: 978-1-957956-85-5 (sc)
ISBN: 978-1-957956-86-2 (e)

Rev. date: 02/27/2023

DEDICATION

This book is dedicated to all young pastors serving in God's Vineyard, to those who intend to join the Gospel Ministry, and to church members who value and cherish their church membership.

ACKNOWLEDGEMENTS

Firstly, I thank God deeply for affording me forty-two years of His precious time in the gospel ministry.

Secondly, I thank my dear wife, Penina Dube, who has been a true helper in gospel ministry and during the writing this book.

Thirdly, I thank my five children—Sibongile, Forward, Londiwe, Patience, and Dorcas—whom God gave as part of my parental development.

Fourthly, Lastly, I thank those whom I rubbed shoulders with during my entire ministry.

PREFACE

I have had the honor of reading the manuscript of Pastor Joseph K. Dube's book. The title, "If I were to do it again," is fascinating because all of us feel that way when we reflect on where we have been.

The book is a light read, allowing the reader to focus on words of wisdom from a tested servant of God. The book also has the advantage of being small and portable, thus allowing one to carry as a constant reminder of the pitfalls and landmines to be aware of and to avoid.

Here is a book that all young pastors should read as they begin their ministry. I recommend this book as a primer for the first-year theology students, particularly those who plan to serve God in African contexts. It is a must read for those who are beginning their ministerial assignment.

Personally, I have been blessed by Pastor Joseph K. Dube's reflections on many areas of ministry. I too wish I could begin again.

Zebron Masukume Ncube, D. Min.
Retired pastor, leader, administrator, and professor.

CONTENTS

CHAPTER 1

INTRODUCTION: CALL TO GOSPEL MINISTRY

When a person begins any type of work, he/she tends to have much bookish knowledge and little or no experience at all. Because of the importance of experience during our generation of ministry, the Adventist Church organisation found it necessary that when a pastor began the work of the gospel ministry he worked under a senior ordained pastor as his mentor.

This was true for me. I worked under two mentors. My first mentor was Pastor P. T. Chimwedzi, at Highfields in Harare, from January to June 1964. Pastor Chimwedzi taught me the importance of time management, especially in conducting funerals and weddings. As a result of his example, I have never been late in most of my appointments, except when I had to attend to an emergency prior to the appointment.

My second mentor was Pastor Judge Dube in Lupane District of Matebeleland North from January 1965 to December 1967. Pastor Dube taught me the importance of leading by example. The old secular concept portrayed the leader as one sitting on a rocking chair in a closed office. However, for Pastor Dube, Christian leadership which Jesus portrayed was that of being leading by example. Jesus mingled with people and walked among them.

What I am sharing here is drawn from serving God for forty-two years, two of which I served as a literature evangelist. One of the most powerful ways of sharing knowledge is through books because it has permanence. I hope and trust that after reading this book, you will have gained some new insights.

There are different ways by which God calls humankind to different callings. In Ephesians 4:11-12, God called some to be apostles, some prophets, some evangelists, and some pastors and teachers. The purpose of which was for the equipping of the saints for the work of ministry to edify the body of Christ, the church.

In my view, while all lines of callings come from God, the highest calling is the call to be a pastor. "Then He said to them, 'Follow me, and I will make you fishers of men'" (Matt 4:19). The highest science is that of calling sinners to Jesus Christ.

Pastoral work is not just a profession but a sacred calling. The gospel minister stands between God and humankind. The minister's duties are to uplift Christ, educate people by the scriptures, and prepare them for the second coming of Jesus as King of Kings and Lord of Lords. "Son of man, I have made you a watchman for the house of Israel; therefore hear a word from My mouth, and give them warning from Me" (Ezekiel 3:17 NKJV).

It is said of Elijah: "So he departed from there, and found Elisha the son of Shaphat, who *was* plowing *with* twelve yoke *of oxen* before him, and he was with the twelfth. Then Elijah passed by him and threw his mantle on him. And he left the oxen and ran after Elijah, and said, "Please let me kiss my father and my mother, and *then* I will follow you. And he said to him, 'Go back again, for what have I done to you?' So *Elisha* turned back from him, and took a yoke of oxen and slaughtered them and boiled their flesh, using the oxen's equipment, and gave it to the people, and they ate. Then he arose and followed Elijah, and became his servant" (1 Kings 19:19-21, NKJV). The act of Elisha meant to forget all and be geared to the single calling from God.

If a person is called by God to the gospel ministry, nobody or circumstance can remove him from the gospel ministry's calling. Years ago, a man married to a teacher and having a well-paying job, received a gospel call from God in his heart. He voiced out the call to the appropriate officers of the Mission Field (Conference). The officers accepted his desire to train as a gospel minister. Arrangements were made for him to go to Solusi College (now University) for training. He quickly resigned from his well-paying job. His intention was to leave his wife behind in Bulawayo for a one school term period as a notice to the Ministry of Education.

When the officers of the Mission Field were informed of this arrangement, they refused him to go to Solusi because of leaving his wife behind for three months. There was no negotiation. The man became very disappointed. Because he had left his previous job, he was forced to looked for a new job elsewhere. Fortunately, he found a job at West Nicholson near Gwanda.

Initially, he thought of putting off the call to the gospel ministry. However, ultimately, a way was open for him to go for theological training at Solusi. Truly, this man was called to the ministry by God, as Jeremiah was. *"For behold, I am calling All the families of the kingdoms of the north," says the Lord; "They shall come and each one set his throne At the entrance of the gates of Jerusalem, Against all its walls all around, And against all the cities of Judah" (Jer. 1:15, NKJV).* Today we have the blessing of the services of Dr Richard Sithole in the Seventh-day Adventist Church. He has served the church as pastor, university registrar, professor, and missionary to Angola.

This example shows the way a call to gospel ministry was understood in the past. A man could not afford to not have his wife live with him for three months, even while doing theological training. Today, however, pastors in full-time service can work for a year away from their families. Surely, things have changed. I defer judgment to the reader on this development.

CHAPTER 2

NEED FOR AN EDUCATED MINISTRY

While it is true that God can use anyone who is consecrated and devoted, regardless of educational qualifications, the society that one is called to serve is dynamic, not static. I remember years ago, a pastor with minimal pastoral training served churches and companies in a district designated as a tourist destination area.

One Sabbath morning when the pastor visited one small company, Seventh-day Adventist tourists came to worship at that company. When the pastor saw the women tourist visitors coming to the gathering wearing pants, he quickly met them and refused them the right to attend church services. He cited Deuteronomy 22:5 to prove his refusal: *"A woman shall not wear anything that pertains to man, nor shall a man put on a woman's garments for all who do so are an abomination to the Lord your God."* Peacefully, the visitors left and returned to their hotel.

Of course, later the company was organized into a church and the district had a pastor with higher academic and professional training. Incidentally, the same tourists that visited the church twelve years before came to the Sabbath worship dressed as they had before—this time with fear due to their experience.

On arrival, they were given a warm welcome by the pastor. After the church service, they related their previous ordeal. The pastor went on to apologize for what had happened due to the former pastor's cultural worldview. The visitors accepted the apology and donated some money towards the church's building project.

Ellen G. White makes the statement "an uneducated worker with consecration can do the work of God but the educated worker with consecration can do the work in a better way" (*Education, p. 172*). Elsewhere this author says, "Higher than the human thought can reach, is God's ideal for His people" (*Messages to Young People, p. 173*). While God uses both educated and uneducated workers who are consecrated to their calling, He expects more from the one who is educated.

The example of Dr Million Booni is one of great interest to me. His preaching eloquence has taken him to many places, both local and overseas. As a lay preacher, the East Zimbabwe Conference in Harare, Zimbabwe, made him a pastor and later ordained him with no formal pastoral training. He has addressed large gatherings at camp meetings in his mother tongue, Shona, because of limitations in English proficiency. Yet, because of his consecration and communicative preaching skills, Solusi University conferred him an Honorary Degree on March 29, 2003.

In 1965, Dr Russell. L. Staples, then principal of Solusi College, made a challenge to theology students to the fact that 'the church in Africa now needs an educated ministry." Most of us who had taken post primary and Junior Certificate (tenth grade) ministerial courses did not understand him. Later, he announced that in years to come no-one was going to be accepted for training in the ministry without five Ordinary Level certificate. It did not make sense then, but today I see the fulfilment of Dr Staples' statement. Solusi University has continued to meet that need for the gospel ministry.

In any congregation that one stands to preach, there are educated members people, even in the most remote areas like Binga, Plumtree, Beitbridge, Muzarabani, to name a few. We are called to minister to a highly literate and technological generation.

At the age of sixty-six in 2004, I had given forty-two years of service in pastoral ministry. I could have given one or two years more, but without computer skills, I felt I was depriving my church members who showed more computer knowledge than me. Besides, computers were becoming a necessary tool for every pastor.

God has chosen his workers at different times and for different times. Some were chosen to pioneer the work of the gospel ministry, some to build the work on the foundation laid by the pioneers, and others will be called to finish God's work. A question may be asked, which group is more important among the three? The truth is that no one group is more important than the others.

In Jesus' parable of the Laborers in the Vineyard in Matthew 20:1, 15, we are all called to build the church of God at different times. Let us all look forward with confidence that we will wear crowns in the graduation school of heaven.

> Again, Ellen G. White says, "If it were possible for us to attain to a full understanding of God and His word there would be for us no further discovery of truth, no greater knowledge, no further development, God would cease to be supreme, and man would cease to advance. Thank God, that it is not the case. Since God is infinite, and in Him are all the treasuries of wisdom we may throughout eternity be ever searching, ever learning, yet never exhaust the

riches of His wisdom, His goodness, nor His power" (*Education, p. 172*).

Realizing my own need for further education, I pursued long distance learning by attending what was called "nigh school." However, things did not work well because of commitments to my extended family. As a result, I experienced financial constraints. My comfort is in the hope of the eternal heavenly education where we shall explore through ceaseless ages the science of all sciences—the cross.

CHAPTER 3

TEAM MINISTRY

When a pastor and his wife are both dedicated to the work of the Gospel Ministry, the work of the pastor becomes enjoyable, fruitful, and a blessing to the church members as well. A good team ministry starts at the choosing of a life partner by the young pastor.

I learned from the pioneers the needed qualities for a partner. Two qualities stood out distinctly—a "committed" member and one who is "attractive." To these qualities shared to us by pioneers, we added formal education and home industry. Today when we consider the 21st century needs, we realize in addition to the list above, the need for academic and professional qualifications.

Our understanding of truth is always progressive while truth itself does not change. I was impressed by the team ministries of Dr and Mrs O. T. Gutu, Dr and Mrs Joel Musvosvi, and Dr and the late Mrs Solomon Maphosa, just to name the few. Also included is Dr and Mrs Jeffrety B. Sibanda, especially when conducting wedding ceremonies. I have from time to time urged twenty-first ministers to have their wives upgrade themselves academically. This will make both the pastor and his spouse enjoy the work of gospel ministry.

Nothing is disheartening than seeing young ministers

engaging in their ministry without the support of their wives. Indeed, some see the work of gospel ministry as the calling of the husband only. Husbands travel alone, even to assignments that would have required the attendance of their spouses. The presence of the pastor's wife will at times greatly increase his effectiveness in reaching out, especially to the female audiences, who may need a special ministry that only a pastor's wife can give.

This is particularly more possible with the provisions of cars, a privilege which was not readily available during our time. The church members are blessed by the blending of the pastor and his wife. "Two *are* better than one, because they have a good reward for their labor. For if they fall, one will lift up his companion. But woe to him *who is* alone when he falls, For *he has* no one to help him up" (*Ecclesiastes 4:9-10, NKJV*).

When I reflect in my ministry, I regret that I failed to utilize my wife as I should have. She could have been helpful in providing guidance in the choice of topics as one who was in touch with my congregation and could more clearly perceive their needs. We could have also partnered in lesson presentations in areas she was gifted in. Furthermore, a pastor's wife can provide helpful insights on the sermon delivery as part of the congregation.

Many ministers' wives have their own areas of giftedness, and this could greatly increase the pastor's effectiveness. Not only is this helpful in ministry, but it boosts their family life. As they partner, they also grow together.

God has particularly gifted women with an amazing intuitive ability. Early in my ministry, my wife surprised me with an unusual request. She suggested that we purchase a pair of barbing clippers, so that we could cut each other's hair and save on going to the salon. I humbly accepted the request. Looking back now, we have saved a lot as we have used these clippers for the past thirty years.

Young ministers who do not make it a priority to build a

team ministry deprive themselves of a fulfilling ministry and a complete one for their congregations. Ministry should not be a solo venture. It requires the input of both husband and wife. When her input is lacking, the pastor's ministry lacks wholesomeness.

CHAPTER 4

WHAT TO GUARD IN THE MINISTRY

While it is true that the call to gospel ministry is a call to a lifetime, it is also an ideal to aspire towards. "But Jesus said to him, 'No one, having put his hand to the plow, and looking back, is fit for the kingdom of God'" (*Luke 9:62, NKJV*).

There are three very sensitive areas in which gospel workers should guard jealously: (1) immoral sexual behaviour, (2) misappropriation of trust funds, and (3) disloyalty to the higher organisations.

While it is a fundamentally honorable for a minister to marry, that process begins at the courtship stage. No young man should court more than one fiancé at a time. Many talented and promising young ministers have failed to manage this stage and ended up dropping out of the gospel ministry.

A young minister who cherishes an immoral behavior will always have this tendency even when he is old. A minister should be exemplary, not only in married life but also during courtship. While other failures can be tolerated, moral fall cannot be overlooked. Paul admonishes us to "flee sexual immorality. Every sin that a man does is outside the body, but he who commits sexual immorality sins against his own body" (*1 Corinthian 6:18, NKJV*).

When a minister is found to have committed the sin of adultery, the employing organization is left without any other option than to terminate his duties as a gospel minister. He may later serve God in other lines of God's cause. This is not only helpful to preserve the sanctity of the ministry, but also the sanctity of life.

The second area for a gospel minister to guard against is misappropriation of trust funds. Nobody is allowed to temper with trust funds. The big temptation is usually to use the money and pay later—I Owe You (IOU). While this is usually done in secret, financial mismanagement is published publicly when encountered. As as a result, it to damages one's reputation.

I was once caught in this web in a way I cannot explain and was suspended for three months. Within one week, all my district treasurer's books were confiscated for audit. When the audit report came out, it read thus: "The amount of the missing money was mistaken, not a habit." I was exonerated and within a month I was reinstated.

I thank God for that good report. The adage goes, *"it is not a mistake to make the first mistake; but it is a mistake to repeat the same mistake."*[1] If one has any financial problems, church policy allows for a one-month salary advance from the employing organization; yet the best counsel given to all is to live within our income.

When the former Matabeland-Mindlands Field was divided into two fields— Central Zimbabwe Field and West Zimbabwe Field—there were about seven pastors who had been put out of the gospel ministry because of alleged acts of misappropriating trust funds. If my memory serves me well, all those ministers who were reinstated into the gospel

---

[1] In a letter signed by H. M. Mafu, President, West Zimbabwe Conference, dated May 6, 2003.

ministry were later dismissed for the second time for the same reasons.

The third area a Seventh-day Adventist gospel worker needs to guard against is disloyalty to the higher organisation. This means understanding and following the organizational set up. All district pastors and departmental directors are answerable to the Conference president. The local Conference is answerable to the Union Conference, which is answerable to the Division, which is answerable to the General Conference, the highest body of the Seventh-day Adventist Church in the whole world.

The tendency for those who are more educated may be to undermine those placed in leadership positions. A situation may exist where the district pastor is tempted to look down upon the Conference officer. In the Seventh-day Adventist Church, the system of ascending and descending loyalty. This makes loyalty a mutual requirement. For the system to flow, there needs to be mutual respect among gospel workers, regardless of the age, level of service, or educational qualification. Besides, there are no promotions or demotions in the Seventh-day Adventist Church but transfers of functions or posts.

In 1986, the then West Zimbabwe Field hosted a city-wide crusade in Bulawayo conducted by the late Randy Stafford, an African American evangelist. All district pastors were called to meet the evangelist at the then Zambesi Union Mission headquarters to make all the preparations for the crusade.

Pastor Stafford laid down all the rules and procedures to be followed. One of our district pastors did not agree with Stafford on certain areas. After presenting his arguments repeatedly, the evangelist silenced the arguing pastor by stating: "Please mind to whom you are speaking." He went on to explain what he meant: "You are all my subordinates in all the planning of this crusade; this is in accordance with the hierarchies of our church organisation." Arguably, Stafford could have stated this differently.

Although Messianic, the principle of respect is imbedded in John 3:30— "He must increase, and I decrease." Whoever is in position of leadership is due respect. No-one is perfect in leadership; therefore, cultivating room for advice and counsel is important. "So Moses heeded the voice of his father-in-law and did all that he had said" (Exodus 18:24, NKJV).

On matters that don't require boards and executive committees to vote, the leader is allowed to make a final decision. Abraham Lincoln, former President of America, once said, "Don't be afraid of people who criticise you, but be afraid of people who flatter you."

No organisation can function without leaders; neither can there be leaders without people. When workers give each other due respect, there will be smooth function of the organisation like the human body. A pastor who gives respect to those above him will enjoy ministry and will serve long in gospel ministry.

CHAPTER 5

LEADING BY EXAMPLE

Work of ministers of the gospel is to love people, mingle with people, meet their needs, and tell share the good news of the gospel.

Pastor Peter Nyathi used to tell us during our workers meeting: "If the district pastor does not believe in the program at his hands, the same will happen to his church members." The General Conference votes objectives and resolutions from time to time, and all these are passed to the local church through the official channels for implementation. The key person is the district pastor.

A story is told of a man who took a few boys to the swimming pool to train them how to swim. They arrived at the swimming pool, and he began to give the boys lessons on swimming. After he had finished lecturing, he commanded the boys to jump into the pool and swim. After considerable of time, no-one jumped into the pool. The trainer wondered at the hesitancy of the boys to jump into the pool. Then one boy said to him: "Could you please demonstrate to us yourself." The teacher was left without any option, except to jump into the pool. Once in the pool, he was able to influence all the boys to jump in and swim. Church members are not interested in the "Do this" but are interested in the "Do as I do."

One area a good pastor is to humbly guard by the grace of God, is his family life. His should be a family where children value the faith of the church. I have emulated Pastor Jonathan Mathaba Dube's family where children were taught to appreciate their parent's faith.

The shepherdess plays a major role in bringing up children. When children are at the stage of choosing careers, they need fundamental guidance. My wife and I spoke to our children about matters of marriage, our faith, and choosing careers in harmony with our faith. We gave them opportunities to ask questions, and we tried to genuinely respond to those questions without projecting judgment.

I have discovered that when children get to the stage of finding a job, they are tempted to prefer well-paying jobs at the expense of Sabbath-keeping. When they asked us, for example, about careers and serving in the military, my wife and I could only tell them to weigh matters and choose for themselves between eternal life and eternal death.

I remember one day when my son, Forward, went for an interview for an advertised job. After the interview, the man in charge of the interview told my son that he had made it, and that he could come to work the following Monday. This was good news to a job seeker. However, before he left, my son asked the man how many days he was to work per week. The man replied, "You will work Monday to Friday, but when there is demand of work, you will be asked to work overtime on Saturday."

My son told the man that he could not work on Sabbath because it was against his faith. The interviewer then asked my son to choose between his job and his faith. Without hesitation, he responded by saying he was prepared to lose his new job than risking his faith.

When he came home and related the story, my heart was uplifted. Prov. 22:6 says, "Train up a child in the way he should go, And when he is old he will not depart from it." Investing in your children will bring great rewards in later years (*NKJV*).

The other area a good minister is to guard against borrowing money from church members. When you borrow money, you are happy like a person going to a wedding; but when you go back to repay, you are like a person going to a funeral. It is below the dignity of a gospel minister to borrow money from church members. It makes the minister lose credibility.

One strongest concept of Christian leadership is to lead by example. May we as ministers of the gospel be sensitive to Paul's words: "But I discipline my body and bring *it* into subjection, lest, when I have preached to others, I myself should become disqualified" (1 Cor 9:27, NKJV).

CHAPTER 6

ON TRANSFERS

While ministers are apostle who move from place to place, from time to time, humanly speaking, they do not like to be transferred. The only exception is when the move is a call to a higher office position.

I was ordained to the gospel ministry after serving for five years. I was ordained at Hanke Mission in 1968 by Pastor Merle Mills, then president of the Trans-Africa Division, headquartered in Harare. In his charge to me, he said: "We are today ordaining you into the gospel ministry, the work which will make you move from place to place, and that will be done by God, and God will do it through the Field Executive Committee. Yours will be your Bible, Hymn Book, and Pamphlet."

The words of Pastor Mills helped me to accept any transfer at any time. I remember my first transfer came after serving six months in Highfields, Harare, to Mpopoma, Bulawayo. Since that time my wife and I were transferred twelve times in our ministry. Moving can be a blessing to the minister as well as to church members. For that reason, a good minister should learn to adapt himself to any situation.

A lack of team spirit can make transferring difficult. A pastor was put in a district, but his wife did not like the place for personal reasons. When word got to the conference president, the couple was reassigned elsewhere. Still the wife was not happy in the new district. Finally, the pastor and his wife left pastoral ministry and took up another line of work. My assessment is that the problem began at the stage of courtship. She did not have the qualities of being a shepherdess.

In 1979 we were transferred from Gadza in the Gokwe area to Plumtree. The transfer was like from Cape to Cairo. I had never been to Plumtree. What I recalled at the time was only the words of a song on radio in Kalanga, "Ndakaloyiwa" (*I have been bewitched*). This brought me fears.

We prayed about this transfer. My wife reminded me of the word of the charge to me at my ordination. She again reminded me of the words of the song, "Anywhere with Jesus I can safely go." So, we finally accepted the transfer. Truthfully, there is no district that we enjoyed our ministry at as the District of Plumtree. We found the Kalanga people there to be very courteous and honest. They would never pass without greeting you.

We arrived at Plumtree at five in the late afternoon and off-loaded our luggage. Early the next morning, an old lady greeted us in Kalanga, saying, "Mabuyani!" ("*Good morning*"). Not knowing the language, I answered, "Sibuye izolo"), meaning we arrived yesterday. She stood there for quietly, and then said, "I am greeting you in the language of the people of Plumtree."

Long leave the people of Plumtree!

One mistake I have noticed during my forty-two years of ministry is that many people including pastors do not make it their policy to keep their membership where they attend weekly. The church manual says that if a person is settled in a new place, after six months, he or she should transfer membership.

I have encountered many problems with members wanting to get married. Church policy in Zimbabwe says marriage banns should be publicized where one holds membership. It happens that a person can work in South Africa for six years while having membership at Sogwala S.D.A. Church in Lower Gwelo. It becomes a problem for the Sogwala Church in Zimbabwe to publicize the marriage banns. The Sogwala Church may just hold the membership but not know the current spiritual condition of the individual. In such a situation, the Sogwala Church may have to ask for a clearance letter from the church where the individual has been attending as a visitor during those six years. This becomes a long process.

People who are not concerned about church membership deprive the church of their service as they may not hold church office, exercise their voting rights, or support the church financially. This challenge may be reduced if members are encouraged to take their names with them early. "For this reason I will not be negligent to remind you always of these things, though you know and are established in the present truth" (*2 Peter 1:12, NKJV*).

CHAPTER 7

PROJECTION IN NEW DISTRICT

When pastoring Pelandaba SDA Church in Bulawayo, whose membership was over 500, it consisted of the following classes of people:

- School teachers   27
- Managers   4
- Nurses   5
- Secretaries   7
- Accountants   11
- Pensioners   11
- Motor mechanics   3
- Carpenters   2
- Electricians   3
- Drivers   3

This cross-section of members presented the challenge to develop and communicate a vision that embraced everyone. Dr Zebron Ncube visited me one Sabbath and requested to conduct a survey where a group of theology students could participate in asking questions while he interviewed me on my experience as a district pastor.

Dr Ncube asked me a question which challenged me to think big about my ministry and even think about writing a book. He asked me how I projected myself in the new district. As I sought clarification on the question, he went on to ask how I made sure that my church members saw my focus and the direction of my leadership.

It was from interview that I began to develop strategies for my districts. As they say, "first impression makes lasting impressions." Whenever I got to a new district, I made it a policy to preach three sermons in successive Sabbaths to the entire district. The following is a sample of the sermon outline that I preached in every new district.

The Purpose of the Cities of Refuge

Main Text: Joshua 20:1-6, Numbers 35:9-34

Preaching 1. Cities built to save accidental killers
- The church for all sinners, regardless of colour, race, or nationality
- Elders/leaders to welcome all who come to seek refuge sincerely
- Church to be safe for sinners to seek help in church (Joshua 20:6).

Preaching 2. Unique Great Commission of the Church

- The gospel mandate (Matt 28:19-20)
- Three angels' messages (Rev 14:6-10)
- Church business (Matt 4:19)
- Extending God's kingdom of grace.

- Two major programs of the church: inreach and outreach

Preaching 3. Divine method of supporting the Gospel

- God owns all (Malaki 3:8-10; Lev 27:30-33; Ps. 24:1.
- Importance of being stewards (Gen. 1:28, 1 Cor 4:2) Blessing of returning tithes & offerings (Malachi 3:10)

Each time I visited a new church I always inquired as to when the church was established and who were the pioneers. One Sabbath I visited a company which had existed for twenty years, but still worshipping under a tree. I challenged the worshipers to think big about the name of God and the importance of a church building which should bring glory to God. "And let them make, me a sanctuary that I may dwell among them" (Ex 25:8). Any lack in God's church is a contradiction to God as Provider. When your church members know your focus, they follow your direction. In three years, a church building was erected to the glory of God. If you work on people, God will work on church buildings.

A survey was taken on church members' participation in church activities. Results were as follows:

- 10% are always active regardless.
- 40% are interested but lake the "know how."
  - Some wait to be given a chance.
  - Some are shy.
  - Others lack the know-how.
- 50% are spectators only.
  - They need motivation.

According to Proverbs 29:18, "Where there is no vision the people perish." The following explain what vision is:
- Being able to see the future
- Being able to assess the present in view of the future.
- Being alert to opportunities
- Being able to make people see what you see

CHAPTER 8

PASTOR'S VISITS TO MEMBERS

While it is impossible for the district pastor to serve all the churches equally, it is his duty to make every effort to visit his churches and companies at least once a year or as often as the needs arise.

One day I found myself in a place I had never dreamed of because I had to attend the funeral of my relative. I usually make it a policy to find out about the presence of Seventh-day Adventists in any place I put my foot on. I certainly was introduced to few members of our church.

I asked them who their church pastor was. They showed ignorance as to who he was, only that they knew the place where the district pastor traditionally stayed. I asked them if they had been long in that district to know if in the last three or four years the pastor visited the church. Sadly, when I asked them if they attended camp meetings, they informed me that only a few older people did.

In another instance, a literature evangelist accompanied me on my first familiarization visit to one remote group of companies. On our arrival, the church members welcomed us in a way that showed they missed the presence of a district pastor. During the afternoon activities, I invited all church treasurers to hand me the trust funds they had received. I was shocked by the amount of silver coins they brought. I soon realized when checking the receipt books that the offering had not been collected for several months.

As a sign of good gesture, our host had prepared sour milk (*amasi*) to carry home with us. Due to the volume of coins, we politely declined the offer as we could not afford to carry extra baggage. We left the container full of milk.

Familiarization visits to all churches and companies is very important to any minister who has the work of the ministry at heart and desires to know his flock well. There is a saying in Ndebele: *"Ukwazi umuntu yikwazi ekhaya lakhe."* It means knowing the person without knowing his home is not enough. Paul the missionary to the Gentiles had four missionary journeys. The first was on church planting and the rest were on following up on his congregations to find out how they were doing in their Christian walk. There is no substitute for pastoral care through visitation.

Pastoral visits should not only be general but specific as well. Every member is important. Nothing should replace a pastoral visit.

A pastor with 3,000 members in his district decided to visit all his members one by one, following the church register. One day he tried visiting a young man who was a temporal teacher in a rural school but did not find. He left a note about his visit.

When the young man came home at the end of the month and learned that the pastor had visited him, he felt touched that the man of God should consider him worth to give such a personal visit. He then personally visited the pastor and later renewed his commitment to attend church. He began returning tithes and offerings, even though the pastor had not brought up the subject.

In his words the young man said, "What am I to be known and visited among 3,000 baptised members?"

Pastors in active service, do your part and God will do his part. "In the morning sow your seed, And in the evening do not withhold your hand; For you do not know which will prosper, Either this or that, Or whether both alike will be good" (*Ecclesiastes 11:6, NKJV*).

CHAPTER 9

PLACE OF THE BIBLE

While in active service as a pastor, I must confess that I did not read the whole Bible and the Spirit of Prophecy books as much as I should have.

I have discovered that there are several methods of studying the Bible. The two that I have followed are (1) systematic method—studying book by book to discover what the Bible teaches. (2) topical method—studying general topics. When I tried the systematic method, I failed to do all sixty-six books of the Bible. I finally opted for the topical method, which does not require much concentration.

For many years I used to wonder how planes and ships can travel where there are no roads. One day I got in contact with a pilot and asked my long burning question. When the pilot told me that the number one instrument was the compass, I was hundred percent satisfied. Realizing the importance of the compass, I concluded that we could use the Bible as our spiritual compass. The four cardinal directions of the compass are changeless, just as the Bible truths do not change. Only our understanding of Bible truths is always progressive.

All successful pilots know the compass and the rest of the instruments surrounding the compass from A to Z. It is required of Christians, certainly pastors, to know the

Scriptures. Jesus observed: "You search the Scriptures, for in them you think you have eternal life; and these are they which testify of Me" (*John 5:39, NKJV*). The Greek in this verse may suggest two meanings—a statement of fact (indicative) or a statement of command (imperative). Either way, the point is that knowing Jesus means knowing the Scriptures. This was predicted earlier in Psalm 40:7: "Then I said, behold I come in the scroll of the book, it is written of me."

The Apostle Paul said: "All Scripture *is* given by inspiration of God, and *is* profitable for doctrine, for reproof, for correction, for instruction in righteousness, that the man of God may be complete, thoroughly equipped for every good work" (*2 Timothy 3:1–17, NKJV*).

Scripture is profitable for doctrine, reproof, correction, instruction, and that the man of God may be complete and equipped. We must therefore study the Bible ". . . precept upon precept, line upon line, line upon line, here a little thee a little" (Isaiah 28:10).

Fellow gospel ministers, it is profitable to study the entire Bible, preferably yearly as I intimated earlier. If we do this, we have the assurance: "But the Helper, the Holy Spirit, whom the Father will send in My name, He will teach you all things, and bring to your remembrance all things that I said to you" (*John 14:26, NKJV*).

A person is only reminded of things one knew in the past. A good medical doctor is the one who knows the medicines and gives the right medicine to patients. I urge you to be men of the Book and use it as your spiritual compass.

CHAPTER 10

ROLE OF SPIRIT OF PROPHECY

While the Seventh-day Adventist Church was born out of an intense study of prophecy, it was also guided by the spirit of prophecy.

I have discovered during my forty-two years of active ministry that there are church members who do not believe in the Spirit of Prophecy—the writings of Ellen G. White. There are also those who go to extremes in their use of the books of Sister White.

To those who do not believe in her books, let me draw this analogy. There is no complete history of the independence of South Africa without the name of Nelson Mandela. Similarly, there can never be a complete history of the Seventh-day Adventist Church without the name of Ellen G. White.

Thankfully, some have made their U-turn and while others are still on their way. Ellen G. White repeatedly said the Bible is the greater light and her writings are the lesser light. Those who go to extremes in their interpretation and application of Ellen G. White are in danger of marginalizing themselves. History shows that many groups were formed based on some narrow or extreme use of the teaching of Ellen G. White.

Following is a list of the role of the writings of Ellen G. White (Spirit of Prophecy) in the Seventh-day Adventist Church:

1. They do not take the place of the sixty-six books of the Bible.
2. They exalt the Bible.
3. They attract our minds to the Bible.
4. They express more the truth already known.
5. They amplify truth that is neglected.
6. They simplify truth that is difficult to understand.
7. They give us principles to be applied when studying the Bible and Spirit of Prophecy.

As in any study of the Bible, the general context of all applicable counsels should be studied before conclusions are made. Due consideration should be given to time, place, and the circumstance of the event of the passage. Finally, the reader should discover and draw out timeless principles involved in any specified counsel.

CHAPTER 11

IMPORTANT DATES FOR THE DISTRICT PASTOR

While the district pastor is always on the pulpit feeding his flock with the word of God, he is not able to attend church services in one church three times in succession. The exception is when on arrival in the new district or when conducting evangelistic meeting.

The idea of having the Lords Supper on special days like holidays such as Easter and Christmas, is not ideal. People travel to be with their families and attendance can be compromised.

The first Sabbath of the year is a special day for the district pastor. When possible, the pastor can gather his churches together to review the progress and set goals for the year ahead. It is a good time for the district pastor to communicate his vision for the new year ahead and to think big for God.

The last Sabbath of the year or Christmas Day is time to count God's blessings, especially the blessing of living from January to December. It is time for thanksgiving and for people to give their testimonies. The pastor can challenge students to thank God for their successes and for a second chance to those who might not have done well. He can remind the church that in life we finish something to begin something else.

A good leader will always plan for his flock. He trains and assigns lay preachers to preach in other churches. Those who pastor districts where Conference, Union, Division, and even General Conference personnel attend, can take advantage of their services and assign them to preach or teach. They enjoy being invited, especially when arrangements are made in advance or when their schedules are flexible.

The importance of setting a calendar for the district cannot be underestimated. It creates a sense of predictability because members know ahead of time when the pastor will show up and which guests they will have.

Also, every pastor should take advantage of the calendar of special days and offerings that come from the conference, union, and division. This makes sure that no church falls behind in programs and activities. Adjustments to the calendar are always possible, given the uniqueness of each church's context. After all, setting a calendar for the entire year demonstrates good leadership on the part of the pastor. It also serves to train elders on the importance of planning.

The larger the district, the more the importance of having a detailed calendar to facilitate good management of programs and activities. It relieves a lot of stress and enhances unity among churches in the district. Churches also begin to feel the importance of belonging to the sisterhood of church in the conference and globally.

CHAPTER 12

PASTOR AS CHIEF COMFORTER AT FUNERALS

While the pastor has many important duties to perform, the Church Manual says the moment the pastor hears of the news of death, he should do everything possible to go and comfort the bereaved. The only thing the family needs during bereavement is to be comforted. Jesus spent much of his time healing the sick and comforting the bereaved.

During the eighteen and nineteen centuries, the gospel minister was considered a prominent figure in the community. This was also true in centuries before. A pastor who loves people will not wait to be invited to a funeral of a non-member of his church. He should make it a point to attend funerals in his area regardless of church affiliation.

I will not forget the way how the late Pastor Jim M Phiri was devoted to funerals at Sogwala District in the Lower Gwelo area. When he could not attend the funeral, he arranged for me to assist at the funeral.

Pastor Phiri's exemplary dedication at the funeral was echoed by one kraal head when he was giving a vote of thanks after the funeral. "We people of Sogwala area are blessed with the unspeakable service of Pastor Phiri and Pastor Dube. The way they share duties is marvellous." This remark humbled me.

If the schedule will not permit you to attend, it is advisable to delegate someone to represent you. Besides, it will show the people that you are duty sensitive.

One day when I was sharing the news of the death of Pastor Phiri to Mr. Moy, a non-believer, he was very much shocked to hear the sad news. Mr Moyo said, "Truly, it is not only your church that has experienced this loss but the whole of our area, because Pastor Phiri was a man of God to Christians and non-Christians alike."

Indeed, that is why somebody said you can only measure the tree accurately when the tree is cut down. Jesus ministered to all people. Similarly, let us be ministers to all people. As the old Missionary Volunteer (Adventist Youth) refrain went: "Brighten the corner where you are."

Jesus was an effective comforter at funerals. (John 11:11, 35). He wept. Luke 7:13 says "When the Lord saw her, His heart went out to her, and He said – 'Don't cry.'" Mourners at that funeral were all filled with awe and praised God.

Indeed, people may not make a decision for Christ at an evangelistic meeting, but do so through the ministry of bereavement at a funeral.

CHAPTER 13

ROLE OF A RETIRED PASTOR

While a pastor is a Conference employee, yet upon his retirement he is equal to that of church member and can be chosen to any office of the church.

A retired pastor in a district can be a blessing or a threat both to the district pastor and the church members. God intends that retirees be a blessing where they reside. During my time of active ministry, I worked in two districts that had two retirees each.

The first one, at Sogwala, I had the blessing of Pastor J. N. Ndebele and Pastor Dick Mahlahla in 1969-72. By then I had only six years of experience. The first thing that came to my mind was that I felt too small to be their pastor. After one month, I had learnt that they were saying to me by their actions, "Young Pastor, lead us and we will give you the support you need."

Surely, there are no two persons that are the same. I began tapping into their individual gifts and talents. I discovered that Pastor Dick Mahlahla was a bookworm who had many Spirit of Prophecy books. He knew most of Ellen G. White's books so much that he could tell me the page without opening the book. He also used to be an interpreter at Lower Gwelo camp meetings in the 1950s. I used Pastor J. N. Ndebele for prayer needs and elderly counselling.

Again, I was privileged to work at Luveve Church in Bulawayo from 1996 to 2002. The church also had two retired pastors—Pastor Donkey Manyathela and Pastor Stanford Mahlahla. At this time, I had the experiences I needed. Before my first Sabbath service I visited the two retirees to inform them of the areas I wanted them to assist me in. Just my special visit to them made them feel free to give me any support. Pastor Manyathela had become blind. He lost his eyesight, but God doubled his memory.

In 2000, the Nyamandlovu Church situated about 50 km west of Bulawayo was unable to go to Solusi Camp Meeting because of drought. They voiced their concern only one month before the date of Solusi Camp Meeting. I took their concern with a suggestion to hold a small camp-meeting at Igusi.

The Conference President, Dr H. Mafu, accepted the people's request and suggestions. However, the matter of camp meeting speakers was left to me as the district pastor. I took Pastor Manyathela and one of the elders from my district. Pastor Manyathela was our main speaker. That was one of the best camp meetings I ever had. It left the camp meeting attendees puzzled about whether Pastor Manyathela was a real blindman or he was partially blind, because when those who read Bible verses for him misquoted them, he pointed it out.

Pastor S. Mahlahla was always at standby as interpreter whenever we had visitors who needed English translation. Pastor Mahlahla was gifted in languages and had a good memory of people's names, just like his father, Pastor Dick Mahlahla. Put a person to do the work in the area where he is talented, he will enjoy it and be a blessing to the congregation.

Dear pastors in active service, when God gives you retirees in your districts, see them as a blessing than a threat. To my fellow retirees, let us give those in active service their places. In the words of John, "Let Him increase and I decrease" (John

3:3). Unfortunately, some retirees find it quite a challenge to accept the reality of their walking on the sidewalk.

As retirees, we should gladly accept assignments in any church office that the local church asks us to carry out. This is true in churches that have few church members for to take a church office. However, if there are enough church members to be elected to church office, the retiree should not be given any church office, but act as a consultant of all church officers under the current district pastor.

My appeal is based on Malaki 2:7: "For the lips of a priest should keep knowledge, And *people* should seek the law from his mouth; For he is the messenger of the Lord of hosts" (NKJV). Also, John 12:12 says, "Is not wisdom found among aged, does not long life being understanding."

CHAPTER 14

IMPORTANCE OF CHURCH BUSINESS MEETINGS

While a church business meeting is sometimes less desirable to a pastor, it is a great tool that the pastor can use to advance the cause of God in the district.

Now is the high time that all churches, especially in rural areas, should heed to the importance of conducting church business meetings once a quarter as per the Church Manual. The old Church Manual suggested any other day apart from Sabbath.

The reality is that Sunday has proved not to work well for church business meetings. I have found out that Sabbath afternoon is the best time to conduct a church business meeting. I stand to be challenged here; however, the current Church Manual does not mention a day for the church business meeting.

One Sunday I attended a church business meeting in one old, organised church in Portsmouth, United Kingdom, as an observer. The attendance was six members only. The members were very much worried about the poor attendance. The six members present voted in favour of trying Saturday night because the major objective of the business meeting was for the church to have all the information about the work of the church from time to time.

I developed a system of having a special church board meeting to hear departmental reports before the church business meeting was held. This helped me as the pastor and church officers to preview all departmental reports. This enabled church board members to speak with one voice before the church they serve.

An orderly business meeting dispels suspicion and gives opportunity for all church members to air their views. It also helps to retain confidence in the church leadership of their church.

As part of the church business meeting, I want to speak about the importance of quarterly reports. Any successful business communicates information from the bottom up. Information is received through the reporting system.

There are three types of reports: (1) a report that gives a true reality, (2) a report that misleads, and (3) a report that makes the receiver jump into unnecessary conclusions. Reports should be submitted to the pastor on time for them to serve a useful purpose. This may pose a challenge to rural churches where written reports are not possible due to the lack of electricity and computers. In such situations, the reports are oral.

CHAPTER 15

ORIGINS OF THE AFRICAN SDA CHURCH

While I do not claim to be a historian, the Seventh-day Adventist Church has had many breakaway movements throughout history. However, Adventism in Zimbabwe saw the formation of two breakaway groups.

The first group was the Reformed Seventh-day Adventist Church whose reason for breaking away was over the question of meat eating and of military service (call ups). The second was the African Seventh-day Adventist Church which broke away in 1956 at Makhulambila Church in Lower Gweru rural area. This church has its headquarters at Sogwala, the area under Chief Sogwala. Its members are found in various areas such as Lower Gweru, Zhombe, Shurugwi, Sanyati, Tsholotsho, and Hwange. The membership is over 7,000.

Four reasons were advanced for breaking away.

- That white people supported their orphans overseas with offerings from Africa.
- That the church did not allow polygamy.
- That politics was not allowed in the church.
- That there was need for an indigenous church.

The Bible verse used to frame these views was Acts 17:26: "And He has made from one blood every nation of men to dwell on all the face of the earth and has determined their preappointed times and the boundaries of their dwellings" (NKJV).

The Superintendent for the area was Pastor P. B. Fairchild. Pastor Luphahla was the local and the elders were Ngwabi and Dick Mahlahla to name the few.

This church is not growing but gains membership from the backslidden members of the Seventh-day Adventist Church. It raises confusion among the members of the public to see that there are two Seventh-day Adventist organizations. The oneness of God's church is compromised.

The African SDA Church does not have its own books, such as hymn books, Sabbath School Lessons; instead, it buys its supplies from the Adventist Church's book shops.

CONCLUSION

As I conclude, it reminds me of the title of this book—"If I were to do it again." There are many regrettable blunders I made, many of which were due to ignorance.

Indeed, experience is the best teacher. As I reflect on my 42 years of service, I can only say: Glory be to God the Owner of the Gospel Ministry! Indeed, there is no better calling than this. Let me conclude by sharing a few take home words of wisdom.

- "God's commands are His enablings"—E. G. White
- "We shall take to heaven except our character"—E. G. White
- "Every good worker should leave a dent wherever he labours"—Dr Leonard Masuku
- "Don't be afraid of people who criticise you but be afraid of people who flatter you"—Abraham Lincoln
- "Brighten the corner where you are"—Old Adventist Youth Aim
- The church needs shepherds, not giraffes.
- No wrong corrects another wrong.
- Success is doing things God's way.
- "Pension money is not for buying napkins"—John N. Donga.
- Our understanding of truth is progressive; but truth does not change.

www.ingramcontent.com/pod-product-compliance
Lightning Source LLC
Chambersburg PA
CBHW070943120626
46546CB00004B/1534